Horace Wemyss Smith, Chauncey M Depew

Andreana

Horace Wemyss Smith, Chauncey M Depew

Andreana

ISBN/EAN: 9783337399863

Printed in Europe, USA, Canada, Australia, Japan

Cover: Foto ©ninafisch / pixelio.de

More available books at **www.hansebooks.com**

PROCEEDINGS

OF A

BOARD

OF

GENERAL OFFICERS,

HELD BY ORDER OF

His Excellency Gen. WASHINGTON,

Commander in Chief of the Army of the United States of AMERICA.

RESPECTING

Major JOHN ANDRE,

Adjutant General of the British Army.

SEPTEMBER 29, 1780.

PHILADELPHIA:
Printed by FRANCIS BAILEY, in Market-Street.
M.DCC.LXXX.

EXTRACTS OF LETTERS

from GENERAL WASHINGTON *to the* PRESIDENT *of* CONGRESS.

ROBINSON'S HOUSE, *in the Highlands,*
September 26, 1780.

SIR,

 HAVE the honor to inform Congress that I arrived here yesterday about twelve o'clock, on my return from Hartford. Some hours previous to my arrival, Major-General Arnold went from his quarters, which were this place, and, as it was supposed, over the river to the garrison at West Point, whither I proceeded myself, in order to visit the post. I found General Arnold had not been there during the day; and, on my return to his quarters, he was still absent. In the meantime, a packet had arrived from Lieut. Colonel Jameson, announcing the capture of a John Anderson, who was endeavouring to go to New-York, with several interesting and important papers, all in the hand-writing of General Arnold. This was also accompanied with a letter from the prisoner, avowing himself to be Major John Andre, Adjutant-General to the British army, relating the manner of his capture, and endeavouring to show that he did not come under the description of a spy. From these several circumstances, and information that the General seemed to be thrown into some degree of agitation, on receiving a letter a little time before he went from his quarters, I was led to conclude immediately that he had heard of Major Andre's captivity, and that he would, if possible, escape to the enemy; and accordingly took such measures as appeared the most probable to apprehend him. But he had embarked in a barge, and proceeded down the river, under a flag, to the Vulture ship of war, which lay at some miles below Stony and Verplank's Points. He wrote me a letter after he got on board. Major Andre is not yet arrived, but I hope he is secure, and that he will be here to-day. I have been, and am taking precautions, which I trust will prove effectual, to prevent the important consequences which this conduct, on the part of General Arnold, was intended to produce. I do not know the party that took Major Andre, but it is said that it consisted only of a few militia, who acted in such a manner upon the occasion, as does them the highest honor, and proves them to be men of great virtue. As soon as I know their names, I shall take pleasure in transmitting them to Congress.

PARAMUS, *October* 7, 1780.

SIR,

I HAVE the honor to enclose Congress a copy of the proceedings of a Board of General Officers in the case of Major Andre, Adjutant-General to the British army. This officer was executed, in pursuance of the opinion of the Board, on Monday the 2d instant, at twelve o'clock, at our late camp, at Tappan. Besides the proceedings, I transmit copies of sundry letters respecting the matter, which are all that passed on the subject, not included in the proceedings.

I have now the pleasure to communicate the names of the three persons who captured Major Andre, and who refused to release him, notwithstanding the most earnest importunities and assurances of a liberal reward on his part. Their names are, *John Paulding, David Williams,* and *Isaac Van Wert.*

PROCEEDINGS

OF A

Board of General Officers,

Held by order of his Excellency General WASHINGTON, *Commander in Chief of the Army of the United States of America, respecting Major* ANDRE, *Adjutant-General of the British Army, September the 29th, 1780, at Tappan, in the State of New-York.*

PRESENT:

Major-General Green, President.
Major-General Lord Sterling,
Major-General St. Clair,
Major-General the Marquis la Fayette,
Major-General Howe,
Major-General the Baron de Steuben,
Brigadier-General Parsons,
Brigadier-General Clinton,
Brigadier-General Knox,
Brigadier-General Glover,
Brigadier-General Patterson,
Brigadier-General Hand,
Brigadier-General Huntington,
Brigadier-General Starke,
John Lawrence, Judge-Advocate-General.

MAJOR ANDRE, Adjutant-General to the British army, was brought before the Board, and the following letter from General Washington to the Board, dated Headquarters, Tappan, September 29, 1780, was laid before them, and read.

Gentlemen :

Major Andre, Adjutant-General to the British army, will be brought before you for your examination. He came within our lines in the night, on an interview with Major-General Arnold, and in an assumed character, and was taken within our lines in a disguised habit, with a pass under a feigned name, and with the enclosed papers concealed upon him. After a careful examination, you will be pleased, as speedily as possible, to report a precise state of his case, together with your opinion of the light in which he ought to be considered, and the punishment that ought to be inflicted. The Judge-Advocate will attend to assist in the examination, who has sundry other papers, relative to this matter, which he will lay before the Board.

I have the honor to be, gentlemen,
    Your most obedient and humble servant,
          G. WASHINGTON.

To the Board of General Officers convened at Tappan.

The names of the officers composing the Board were read to Major Andre, and on his being asked whether he confessed the matters contained in the letter from his Excellency General Washington to the Board, or denied them, he said, "in addition to his letter to General Washington, dated Salem, the 24th September, 1780," which was read to the Board, and acknowledged by Major Andre to have been written by him, which letter is as follows:

                    SALEM, *September* 24, 1780.
SIR,

WHAT I have as yet said concerning myself, was in the justifiable attempt to be extricated; I am too little accustomed to duplicity to have succeeded.

I beg your Excellency will be persuaded that no alteration in the temper of my mind, or apprehension for my safety, induces me to take the step of addressing you, but that it is to secure myself from an imputation of having assumed a mean character, for treacherous purposes or self-interest—a conduct incompatible with the principles that actuated me, as well as with my condition in life.

It is to vindicate my fame that I speak, and not to solicit security.

The person in your possession is Major John Andre, Adjutant-General to the British army.

The influence of one commander in the army of his adversary, is an advantage taken in war. A correspondence for this purpose I held; as confidential (in the present instance) with his Excellency Sir Henry Clinton.

To favor it, I agreed to meet upon ground not within posts of either army, a person who was to give me intelligence: I came up in the Vulture man of war, for this effect, and was fetched, by a boat from the shore, to the beach: Being there, I was told that the approach of day would prevent my return, and that I must be concealed until the next night. I was in my regimentals, and had fairly risked my person.

Against my stipulation, my intention, and without my knowledge before hand, I was conducted within one of your posts. Your Excellency may conceive my sensation on this occasion, and will imagine how much more I must have been affected, by a refusal to re-conduct me back the next night, as I had been brought. Thus become a prisoner, I had to concert my escape. *I quitted my uniform*, was passed another way in the night without the American posts to neutral ground, and informed I was beyond all armed parties, and left to press for New York. I was taken at Tarry-Town by some volunteers.

Thus, as I have had the honor to relate, was I betrayed (being Adjutant-General of the British army) into the vile condition of an enemy in disguise within your posts.

Having avowed myself a British officer, I

have nothing to reveal but what relates to myself, which is true on the honor of an officer and a gentleman.

The request I have to make your Excellency, and I am conscious I address myself well, is, that in any rigor policy may dictate, a decency of conduct towards me may mark, that though unfortunate, I am branded with nothing dishonorable, as no motive could be mine but the service of my King, and as I was involuntarily an impostor.

Another request is, that I may be permitted to write an open letter to Sir Henry Clinton, and another to a friend for clothes and linen.

I take the liberty to mention the condition of some gentlemen at Charleston, who being either on parole or under protection, were engaged in a conspiracy against us. Tho' their situation is not similar, they are objects who may be set in exchange for me, or are persons whom the treatment I receive might affect.

It is no less, Sir, in a confidence in the generosity of your mind, than on account of

your superior station, that I have chosen to
importune you with this letter.

I have the honor to be,
    With great respect, Sir,
        Your Excellency's most obedient,
            and most humble servant,
                JOHN ANDRE,
                    Adjutant-General.
His Excellency General Washington,
    &c. &c. &c.

That he came on shore from the Vulture
sloop of war, in the night of the twenty-first
of September instant, somewhere under the
Haverstraw Mountain: That the boat he
came on shore in carried no flag; and that
he had on a surtout coat over his regimentals, and that he wore his surtout coat when
he was taken: That he met General Arnold
on the shore, and had an interview with him
there. He also said, that when he left the
Vulture sloop of war, it was understood that
he was to return that night; but it was then
doubted, and if he could not return, he was
promised to be concealed on shore in a place

of safety, until the next night, when he was to
return in the same manner he came on shore;
and when the next day came, he was solicitous
to get back, and made inquiries in the course
of the day how he should return, when he was
informed he could not return that way, and he
must take the route he did afterwards. He
also said, that the first notice he had of his
being within any of our posts, was, being chal-
lenged by the sentry, which was the first night
he was on shore. He also said, that the evening of the twenty-second September instant,
he passed King's-Ferry, between our posts of
Stony and Verplanck's Points, in the dress he
is at present in, and which he said was not his
regimentals, and which dress he procured, after
he landed from the Vulture, and when he was
within our post; and that he was proceeding
to New-York, but was taken on his way at
Tarry Town, as he has mentioned in his
letter, on Saturday the twenty-third of September instant, about nine o'clock in the
morning.

The following papers were laid before the
Board and shewn to Major Andre, who confessed to the Board, that they were found on

him when he was taken, and said they were concealed in his boot, except the pass:——

A pass from General Arnold to John Anderson, which name Major Andre acknowledged he assumed.

Artillery orders, September 5, 1780.

Estimate of the forces at West-Point and its dependencies, September, 1780.

Estimate of men to man the works at West-Point, &c.

Return of ordnance at West-Point, September, 1780.

Remarks on works at West-Point.

Copy of a state of matters laid before a council of war, by his Excellency General Washington, held the 6th of September, 1780.

A letter signed *John Anderson*, dated September 7, 1780, to Colonel Sheldon,* was also

---

* Lest it should be supposed that Col. Sheldon, to whom the above letter is addressed, was privy to the plot carrying on by General Arnold, it is to be observed, that the letter was found among Arnold's papers, and had been transmitted by Colonel Sheldon, who, it appears from a letter of the 9th of September, to Arnold, which enclosed it, had never heard of John Anderson before. Arnold, in his answer on the 10th, acknowledged that he had not communicated it to him, though he had informed him that he expected a person would come from New-York, for the purpose of bringing him intelligence.

laid before the Board, and shewn to Major Andre, which *he acknowledged* to have been written by *him*, and is as follows:

NEW-YORK, *the 7th Sept.*, 1780.

SIR,

I AM told *my name* is made known to you, and that I may hope your indulgence in permitting me to meet a friend near your out-post. I will endeavour to obtain permission to go out *with a flag*, which will be sent to Dobb's-Ferry on Monday next, the 11th, at twelve o'clock, when I shall be happy to meet Mr. G——.* Should I not be allowed to go, the officer who is to command the escort, between whom and myself no distinction need be made, can speak on the affair.

Let me entreat you, Sir, to favor a matter so interesting to the parties concerned, and which is of so private a nature, that the public on neither side can be injured by it.

---

* It appears by the same letter, that Arnold had written to Mr. Anderson under the signature of Gustavus. His words are, "I was obliged to write with great caution to him, my letter was signed Gustavus, to prevent any discovery, in case it fell into the hands of the enemy."

I shall be happy on my part in doing any act of kindness to you in a family or property concern of a similar nature.

I trust I shall not be detained, but should any old grudge be a cause for it, I shall rather risk that, than neglect the business in question, *or assume a mysterious character* to carry on an innocent affair, and, as friends have advised, get to your lines by stealth. I am, Sir, with all regard,

Your most obedient humble servant,

JOHN ANDERSON.

Col. Sheldon.

Major Andre observed that this letter could be of no force in the case in question, as it was written in New-York, when he was under the orders of General Clinton; but that it tended to prove that it was not his intention to come within our lines.

The Board having interrogated Major Andre about his conception of his coming on shore under the sanction of a flag, he said *that it was impossible for him to suppose he came on shore under that sanction;* and added, that if he came on shore under that sanction, he certainly might have returned under it.

Major Andre, having acknowledged the preceding facts, and being asked whether he had any thing to say respecting them, answered, he left them to operate with the Board.

The examination of Major Andre being concluded, he was remanded into custody.

The following letters were laid before the Board, and read:——Benedict Arnold's letter to General Washington, dated September 25, 1780; Colonel Robinson's letter to General Washington, dated September 25, 1780; and General Clinton's letter, dated 26th September, 1780, (inclosing a letter of the same date from Benedict Arnold,) to General Washington.

ON BOARD THE VULTURE, *Sept.* 25, 1780.

SIR,

THE heart which is conscious of its own rectitude, cannot attempt to palliate a step which the world may censure as wrong; I have ever acted from a principle of love to my country, since the commencement of the present unhappy contest between Great

Britain and the Colonies; the same principle of love to my country actuates my present conduct, however it may appear inconsistent to the world, who very seldom judge right of any man's actions.

I have no favor to ask for myself, I have too often experienced the ingratitude of my country to attempt it; but from the known humanity of your Excellency, I am induced to ask your protection for Mrs. Arnold, from every insult and injury that the mistaken vengeance of my country may expose her to. It ought to fall only on me; she is as good and as innocent as an angel, and is incapable of doing wrong. I beg she may be permitted to return to her friends in Philadelphia, or to come to me, as she may choose: from your Excellency I have no fears on her account, but she may suffer from the mistaken fury of the country.

I have to request that the enclosed letter may be delivered to Mrs. Arnold, and she permitted to write to me.

I have also to ask that my clothes and baggage, which are of little consequence, may be sent to me; if required, their value shall be paid for in money.

I have the honor to be, with great regard and esteem,

>> Your Excellency's most
>> obedient humble servant,
>> B. ARNOLD.

His Excellency General Washington.

N. B. In justice to the gentlemen of my family, Colonel Varick and Major Franks, I think myself in honor bound to declare, that they, as well as Joshua Smith, Esq., (who I know is suspected,) are totally ignorant of any transactions of mine, that they had reason to believe were injurious to the public.

VULTURE OFF SINKSINK, *Sept.* 25, 1780.

SIR,

I AM this moment informed that Major Andre, Adjutant-General of his Majesty's army in America, is detained as a prisoner by the army under your command; it is, therefore, incumbent on me to inform you of the manner of his falling into your hands. He went up with a flag at the request of General Arnold, on public business with him, and had his permit to return by land to New-York. Under these circumstances Major Andre cannot be detained by you, without the greatest violation of flags, and contrary to the custom and usage of all nations, and, as I imagine you will see this matter in the same point of view as I do, I must desire that you will order him to be set at liberty, and allowed to return immediately. Every step Major Andre took was by the advice and direction of General Arnold, even that of taking a feigned name, and of course not liable to censure for it.

I am, Sir,
  not forgetting former acquaintance,
   Your very humble servant,
    BEV. ROBINSON,
     Col. Loyal Americans.

His Excellency General Washington.

NEW-YORK, *Sept.* 26, 1780.

SIR,

BEING informed that the King's Adjutant-General in America has been stopt under Major-General Arnold's passports, and is detained a prisoner in your Excellency's army, I have the honor to inform you, Sir, that I permitted Major Andre to go to Major-General Arnold, at the particular request of that general officer. You will perceive, Sir, by the inclosed paper, that a flag of truce was sent to receive Major Andre, and passports granted for his return: I therefore can have no doubt but your Excellency will immediately direct, that this officer has permission to return to my orders at New-York.

I have the honor to be,
    Your Excellency's most obedient
      and most humble servant,
          H. CLINTON.

His Excellency General Washington.

NEW-YORK, *Sept.* 26, 1780.

SIR,

IN answer to your Excellency's message, respecting your Adjutant-General, Major Andre, and desiring my idea of the reasons why he is detained, being under my passports, I have the honor to inform you, Sir, that I apprehend a few hours must return Major Andre to your Excellency's orders, as that officer is assuredly under the protection of a flag of truce sent by me to him, for the purpose of a conversation which I requested to hold with him relating to myself, and which I wished to communicate through that officer to your Excellency.

I commanded at the time at West-Point, had an undoubted right to send my flag of truce for Major Andre, who came to me under that protection, and having held my conversation with him, I delivered him confidential papers in my own hand-writing, to deliver to your Excellency. Thinking it much properer he should return by land, I directed him to make use of the feigned name of John Anderson, under which he had by my direction come on shore, and gave him my passports to go to the White Plains, on his way to New-York. This officer cannot therefore fail of being immediately sent to New-York, as he was invited to a conversation with me, for which I sent him a flag of truce, and finally gave him passports for his safe return to your Excellency; all which I had then a right to do, being in the actual service of America, under the orders of General Washington, and commanding general at West-Point and its dependencies.

I have the honor to be,
>Your Excellency's most obedient,
>>and most humble servant,
>>>B. ARNOLD.

His Excellency Sir Henry Clinton.

The Board having considered the letter from his Excellency General Washington respecting Major Andre, Adjutant-General to the British Army, the confession of Major Andre, and the papers produced to them, REPORT to his Excellency the Commander in Chief the following facts, which appear to them relative to Major Andre.

First, That he came on shore from the Vulture sloop of war in the night of the twenty-first of September instant, on an interview with General Arnold, in a private and secret manner.

Secondly, That he changed his dress within our lines, and under a feigned name, and in a disguised habit, passed our works at Stony and Verplank's Points, the evening of the twenty-second of September instant, and was taken the morning of the twenty-third of September instant, at Tarry-Town in a disguised habit, being then on his way to New-York; and when taken, he had in his possession several papers, which contained intelligence for the enemy.

The Board having maturely considered these facts, DO ALSO REPORT to his Excellency General Washington, that Major Andre, Adjutant-General to the British army, ought to be considered as a Spy from the enemy, and that agreeably to the law and usage of nations, it is their opinion, he ought to suffer death.

Nathaniel Green, Major-General, President,
Stirling, Major-General,
Ar. St. Clair, Major-General,
La Fayette, Major-General,
R. Howe, Major-General,
Steuben, Major-General,
Samuel H. Parsons, Brigadier-General,
James Clinton, Brigadier-General,
H. Knox, Brigadier-General of Artillery,
John Glover, Brigadier-General,
John Patterson, Brigadier-General,
Edward Hand, Brigadier-General,
J. Huntington, Brigadier-General,
John Starke, Brigadier-General,
John Lawrence, Judge-Advocate-General.

APPENDIX.

Copy of a Letter from Major Andre, Adjutant-General, to Sir Henry Clinton, K. B., &c., &c.

TAPPAN, *Sept.* 29, 1780.

SIR,

OUR Excellency is doubtless already apprized of the manner in which I was taken, and possibly of the serious light in which my conduct is considered, and the rigorous determination that is impending.

Under these circumstances I have obtained General Washington's permission to send you this letter; the object of which is, to remove from your breast any suspicion, that I could imagine I was bound by your Excellency's orders to expose myself to what has hap-

pened. The events of coming within an
enemy's posts, and of changing my dress,
which led me to my present situation, were
contrary to my own intentions, as they were
to your orders; and the circuitous route, which
I took to return, was imposed (perhaps una-
voidably) without alternative upon me.

I am perfectly tranquil in mind, and pre-
pared for any fate to which an honest zeal
for my King's service may have devoted me.

In addressing myself to your Excellency on
this occasion, the force of all my obligations
to you, and of the attachment and gratitude I
bear you recurs to me. With all the warmth
of my heart, I give you thanks for your Excellency's profuse kindness to me; and I send
you the most earnest wishes for your welfare,
which a faithful, affectionate, and respectful
attendant can frame.

I have a mother and three sisters, to whom
the value of my commission would be an object, as the loss of Granada has much affected
their income. It is needless to be more
explicit on this subject; I am persuaded of
your Excellency's goodness.

I receive the greatest attention from his

Excellency General Washington, and from
every person under whose charge I happen to
be placed.

I have the honor to be,
    With the most respectful attachment,
      Your Excellency's most obedient
        and most humble servant,
           JOHN ANDRE,
                Adjutant-General.

(Addressed)
  His Excellency Gen. Sir Henry
    Clinton, K. B., &c., &c., &c.

Copy of a Letter from his Excellency General Washington, to his Excellency Sir Henry Clinton.

          HEAD-QUARTERS, *Sept.* 30, 1780.
SIR,

    IN answer to your Excellency's letter of the 26th instant, which I had the honor to receive, I am to inform you, that Major Andre was taken under such circumstances as would have justified the most summary proceedings against him. I determined however to refer his case to the examination and decision of a Board of General Officers, who have reported on his free and voluntary confession and letters, "That he came on shore from the Vulture sloop of war, in the night of the twenty-first of September instant," &c., &c., as in the Report of the Board of General Officers.

From these proceedings, it is evident Major Andre was employed in the execution of measures very foreign to the objects of flags of truce, and such as they were never meant to authorize or countenance in the most distant degree; and this gentleman confessed with the greatest candor, in the course of his examination, "That it was impossible for him to suppose he came on shore, under the sanction of a flag."

I have the honor to be,
    Your Excellency's most obedient
       and most humble servant,
           G. WASHINGTON.

(Addressed)
  His Excellency Sir Henry Clinton.

APPENDIX.

In this letter Major Andre's of the 29th of September to Sir Henry Clinton was transmitted.

NEW-YORK, *Sept.* 29, 1780.

SIR,

PERSUADED that you are inclined rather to promote than prevent the civilities and acts of humanity, which the rules of war permit between civilized nations, I find no difficulty in representing to you, that several letters and messages sent from hence have been disregarded, are unanswered, and the flags of truce that carried them, detained. As I have ever treated all flags of truce with civility and respect, I have a right to hope, that you will order my complaint to be immediately redressed.

Major Andre, who visited an officer commanding in a district at his own desire, and acted in every circumstance agreeable to his direction, I find is detained a prisoner; my friendship for him leads me to fear he may suffer some inconvenience for want of necessaries; I wish to be allowed to send him a

few, and shall take it as a favor if you will be pleased to permit his servant to deliver them. In Sir Henry Clinton's absence, it becomes a part of my duty to make this representation and request.

I am, Sir,
    Your Excellency's most
        obedient humble servant,
            JAMES ROBERTSON,
                  Lieutenant-General.

His Excellency General Washington.

                  TAPPAN, *Sept.* 30, 1780.
SIR,

I HAVE just received your letter of the 29th. Any delay which may have attended your flags, has proceeded from accident and the peculiar circumstances of the occasion, not from intentional neglect or violation. The letter that admitted of an answer, has received one as early as it could be given with propriety, transmitted by a flag this morning. As to messages, I am uninformed of any that have been sent.

APPENDIX.   33

The necessaries for Major Andre will be delivered to him, agreeably to your request.
I am, Sir,
Your most obedient humble servant,
G. WASHINGTON.

His Excellency Lieut.-Gen. Robertson,
New-York.

NEW-YORK, *Sept.* 30, 1780.
SIR,
FROM your Excellency's letter of this date, I am persuaded the Board of General Officers, to whom you referred the case of Major Andre, cannot have been rightly informed of all the circumstances on which a judgment ought to be formed. I think it of the highest moment to humanity, that your Excellency should be perfectly apprized of the state of this matter, before you proceed to put that judgment in execution.

For this reason, I send his Excellency Lieutenant-General Robertson, and two other gentlemen, to give you a true state of facts, and to declare to you my sentiments and resolutions. They will set out to-morrow, as early as the wind and tide will permit, and wait near Dobb's Ferry for your permission and safe conduct, to meet your Excellency, or such persons as you may appoint, to converse with them on this subject.

I have the honor to be,
    Your Excellency's most obedient
        and most humble servant,
                H. CLINTON.

P. S.—The Hon. Andrew Elliot, Esq., Lieutenant-Governor, and the Hon. William Smith, Chief-Justice of this province, will attend his Excellency Lieutenant-General Robertson.
                H. C.

His Excellency General Washington.

Lieutenant-General Robertson, Mr. Elliot, and Mr. Smith, came up in a flag vessel to Dobb's Ferry, agreeable to the above letter. The two last were not suffered to land. General Robertson was permitted to come on shore, and was met by Major-General Greene, who verbally reported that General Robertson mentioned to him in substance what is contained in his letter of the 2d of October to General Washington.

NEW-YORK, *October* 1, 1780.

SIR,

I TAKE this opportunity to inform your Excellency, that I consider myself no longer acting under the commission of Congress: Their last to me being among my papers at West Point, you, Sir, will make such use of it as you think proper.

At the same time, I beg leave to assure your Excellency, that my attachment to the true interest of my country is invariable, and that I am actuated by the *same principle* which has ever been the *governing rule* of my conduct, in this unhappy contest.

I have the honor to be,
    Very respectfully, your Excellency's
        most obedient humble servant,
            B. ARNOLD.

His Excellency General Washington.

GREYHOUND SCHOONER, FLAG OF TRUCE,
Dobb's FERRY, *Oct.* 2, 1780.

SIR,

A NOTE I have from General Greene, leaves me in doubt if his memory had served him to relate to you, with exactness, the substance of the conversation that had passed between him and myself, on the subject of Major Andre. In an affair of so much consequence to my friend, to the two armies, and humanity, I would leave no possibility of a misunderstanding, and therefore take the liberty to put in writing the substance of what I said to General Greene.

I offered to prove by the evidence of Colonel Robinson, and the officers of the Vulture, that Major Andre went on shore at General Arnold's desire, in a boat sent for him with a flag of truce; that he not only came ashore with the knowledge, and under the protection of the general who commanded in the district, but that he took no step, while on shore, but by the direction of General Arnold, as will appear by the inclosed letter from him to your Excellency. Under these circumstances I could not, and hoped you would not, consider Major Andre as a spy, for any improper phrase in his letter to you.

The facts he relates correspond with the evidence I offer; but he admits a conclusion that does not follow. The change of clothes and name was ordered by General Arnold, under whose direction he necessarily was while within his command. As General Greene and I did not agree in opinion, I wished that disinterested gentlemen of knowledge of the law of war and nations, might be asked their opinion on the subject, and mentioned Monsieur Knyphausen and General Rochambault.

I related that a Captain Robinson had been delivered to Sir Henry Clinton as a spy, and undoubtedly was such; but that it being signified to him that you were desirous that this man should be exchanged, he had ordered him to be exchanged.

I wished that an intercourse of such civilities as the rules of war admit of, might take off many of its horrors. I admitted that Major Andre had a great share of Sir Henry Clinton's esteem, and that he would be infinitely obliged by his liberation; and that if he was permitted to return with me I would engage to have any person you would be pleased to name, set at liberty.

I added that Sir Henry Clinton had never put to death any person for a breach of the rules of war, though he had, and now has, many in his power. Under the present circumstances, much good may arise from humanity, much ill from the want of it. If that could give any weight, I beg leave to add, that your favorable treatment of Major Andre will be a favor I should ever be intent to return to any you hold dear.

My memory does not retain with the exactness I could wish, the words of the letter which General Greene shewed me from Major Andre to your Excellency. For Sir Henry Clinton's satisfaction, I beg you will order a copy of it to be sent to me at New-York.

I have the honor to be,
  Your Excellency's most obedient
   and most humble servant,
    JAMES ROBERTSON.

His Excellency General Washington.

NEW-YORK, *October* 1, 1780.

SIR,

THE polite attention shewn by your Excellency and the gentlemen of your family to Mrs. Arnold, when in distress, demands my grateful acknowledgment and thanks, which I beg leave to present.

From your Excellency's letter to Sir Henry Clinton, I find a Board of General Officers have given it as their opinion, that Major Andre comes under the description of a spy. My good opinion of the candor and justice of those gentlemen leads me to believe, that if they had been made fully acquainted with every circumstance respecting Major Andre, that they would by no means have considered him in the light of a spy, or even of a prisoner. In justice to him, I think it my duty to declare, that he came from on board the Vulture at my particular request, by a flag sent on purpose for him by Joshua Smith, Esq., who had permission to go to Dobb's Ferry, to carry letters, and for other purposes not mentioned, and to return. This was done as a blind to the spy boats. Mr.

Smith at the same time had my private instructions, to go on board the Vulture, and bring on shore Colonel Robinson, or Mr. John Anderson, which was the name I had requested Major Andre to assume; at the same time I desired Mr. Smith to inform him that he should have my protection, and a safe passport to return in the same boat, as soon as our business was completed. As several accidents intervened to prevent his being sent on board, I gave him my passport to return by land. Major Andre came on shore in his uniform, (without disguise,) which with much reluctance, at my particular and pressing instance, he exchanged for another coat. I furnished him with a horse and saddle, and pointed out the route by which he was to return. And as commanding officer in the department, I had an undoubted right to transact all these matters, which, if wrong, Major Andre ought by no means to suffer for them.

But if, after this just and candid representation of Major Andre's case, the Board of General Officers adhere to their former opinion, I shall suppose it dictated by passion and resentment; and if that gentleman should suffer the severity of their sentence, I shall think myself bound, by every tie of duty and honor, to retaliate on such unhappy persons of your army as may fall within my power, that the respect due to flags, and to the law of nations, may be better understood and observed.

I have further to observe, that forty of the principal inhabitants of South Carolina have justly forfeited their lives, which have hitherto been spared by the clemency of his Excellency Sir Henry Clinton, who cannot in justice extend his mercy to them any longer, if Major Andre suffers; which, in all probability, will open a scene of blood at which humanity will revolt.

Suffer me to intreat your Excellency for your own and the honor of humanity and the love you have of justice, that you suffer not an unjust sentence to touch the life of Major Andre.

But if this warning should be disregarded, and he suffer, I call heaven and earth to witness, that your Excellency will be justly answerable for the torrent of blood that may be spilt in consequence.

I have the honor to be, with due respect,
Your Excellency's most obedient
and very humble servant,
B. ARNOLD.

His Excellency General Washington.

TAPPAN, *October* 1, 1780.

SIR,

BUOY'D above the terror of death, by the consciousness of a life devoted to honorable pursuits, and stained with no action that can give me remorse, I trust that the request I make to your Excellency at this serious period, and which is to soften my last moments, will not be rejected.

Sympathy towards a soldier will surely induce your Excellency and a military tribunal, to adapt the mode of my death to the feelings of a man of honor.

Let me hope, Sir, that if aught in my character impresses you with esteem towards me, if aught in my misfortunes marks me as the victim of policy and not of resentment, I shall experience the operation of these feelings in your breast, by being informed that I am not to die on a gibbet.

I have the honor to be,
    Your Excellency's most obedient
        and most humble servant,
           JOHN ANDRE,
        Adj. Gen. to the British Army.
His Excellency General Washington.

The time which elapsed between the capture of Major Andre, which was on the morning of the 23d of September, and his execution, which did not take place till twelve o'clock on the second of October; the mode of trying him; his letter to Sir Henry Clinton, K. B., on the 29th of September, in which he said, "I receive the greatest attention from his Excellency General Washington, and from every person under whose charge I happen to be placed;" not to mention many other acknowledgments which he made of the good treatment he received; must evince that the proceedings against him were not guided by passion or resentment.

The practice and usage of war was against his request, and made the indulgence he solicited, circumstanced as he was, inadmissible.

Published by order of Congress.

CHARLES THOMSON.

Secretary.

EXTRACT *from a* LETTER *which appeared in the Pennsylvania Gazette, dated October* 25, 1780. *The author supposed to be Colonel* HAMILTON, *Aid-de-Camp to General* WASHINGTON.

NEVER, perhaps, did a man suffer death with more justice or deserve it less. The first step he took after his capture, was to write a letter to General Washington, conceived in terms of dignity without insolence, and apology without meanness. The scope of it was to vindicate himself from the imputation of having assumed a mean character, for treacherous or interested purposes, that, contrary to his intention, which was to meet a person for intelligence on neutral ground, he had been betrayed within our posts, and forced into the vile condition of an enemy in disguise, soliciting only, that to whatever rigor policy might devote him, a decency of treatment might be observed due to a person who, though unfortunate, had been guilty of nothing dishonorable. His request was granted in its full extent; for in the whole progress of the affair, he was treated with the most scrupulous delicacy. When brought before the Board of Officers, he met with every mark of indulgence, and was required to answer no interrogatory which could embarrass his feeling.

On his part, while he carefully concealed every thing that might involve others, he frankly confessed all the facts relative to himself; and, upon his confession, without the trouble of examining a witness, the Board made their report. The members of it were not more impressed with the candor and modest firmness, mixed with a becoming sensibility, which he displayed, than he was penetrated with their liberality and politeness. He acknowledged the generosity of the behaviour towards him in every respect, but particularly in this in the strongest terms of manly gratitude. In a conversation with a gentleman who visited him after his trial, he said, he flattered himself he had never been illiberal; but if there were any remains of prejudice in his mind, his present experience must obliterate them.

In one of the visits I made to him (and I saw him several times during his confinement) he begged me to be the bearer of a request to the General, for permission to send an open letter to Sir Henry Clinton. "I foresee my fate," said he, "and though I pretend not to play the hero, or to be indifferent about life, yet I am reconciled to whatever may happen, conscious that misfortune, not guilt, will have brought it upon me. There is only one thing that disturbs my tranquillity. Sir Henry Clinton has been too good to me; he has been lavish of his kindness. I am bound to him by too many obligations, and love him too well, to bear the thought that he should reproach himself, or that others should reproach him, on a supposition that I had conceived myself obliged by his instructions to run the risk I did. I would not for the world leave a sting in his mind, that should embitter his

APPENDIX. 47

future days." He could scarce finish the sentence, bursting into tears in spite of his efforts to suppress them, and with difficulty collected himself enough afterwards to add, "I wish to be permitted to assure him I did not act under this impression, but submitted to a necessity imposed upon me, as contrary to my own inclination as to his orders." His request was readily complied with, and he wrote the letter annexed, with which I dare say you will be as much pleased as I am, both for the diction and sentiment.

When his sentence was announced to him, he remarked, that since it was his lot to die, as there was a choice in the mode, which would make material difference in his feelings, he would be happy, if it were possible to be indulged with a professional death.

He made a second application by letter, in concise but persuasive terms. It was thought this indulgence, being incompatible with the customs of war, could not be granted; and it was therefore determined in both cases to evade an answer, to spare him the sensations which a certain knowledge of the intended mode would inflict.

When he was led out to the place of execution, as he went along he bowed familiarly to all those with whom he had been acquainted in his confinement. A smile of complacency expressed the serene fortitude of his mind. Arrived at the fatal spot, he asked with emotion, "Must I then die in this manner?" He was told it had been unavoidable. "I am reconciled to my fate," said he, "but not to the mode." Soon, however, recollecting himself, he added, "It will be but a momentary pang," and, springing upon the cart, performed the last offices to himself, with a composure that excited the admiration, and melted the hearts of the beholders. Upon being told the final moment was at hand, and asked if he had any thing to say, he answered, "Nothing but to request you will witness to the world that I die like a brave man." Among the extraordinary circumstances that attended him, in the midst of his enemies, he died universally esteemed, and universally regretted.

There was something singularly interesting in the character and fortunes of Andre. To an excellent understanding, well improved by education and travel, he united a peculiar elegance of mind and manners, and the advantage of a pleasing person. It is said he possessed a pretty taste for the fine arts, and had himself attained some proficiency in poetry, music, and painting. His knowledge appeared without ostentation, and embellished by a diffidence that rarely accompanies so many talents and accomplishments, which left you to suppose more than appeared. His sentiments were elevated, and inspired esteem; they had a softness that conciliated affection. His elocution was handsome, his address easy, polite, and insinuating. By his merit he had acquired the confidence of his General, and was making a rapid progress in military rank and reputation. But in the heighth of his career, flushed with new hopes from the execution of a project the most beneficial to his party that could be devised, he is at once precipitated from the summit of prosperity, sees all the expectations of his ambition blasted and himself ruined.

The character I have given of him is drawn partly from what I saw of him myself, and partly from information. I am aware that a man of real merit is never seen in so favorable a light as through the medium of adversity. The clouds that surround him are so many shadows that set off his good qualities. Misfortune cuts down little vanities that, in prosperous times, serve as so many spots in his virtues, and gives a tone of humility that makes his worth more amiable. His spectators, who enjoyed a happier lot, are less prone to detract from its true envy; and are more disposed by compassion to give him the credit he deserves, and perhaps even to magnify it.

I speak not of Andre's conduct in this affair as a philosopher, but as a man of the world. The authorized maxims and practices of war are the sators of human nature. They countenance almost every species of seduction as well as violence, and the General who can make most traitors in the army of his adversary is frequently most applauded. On this scale we acquit Andre, while we could not but condemn him if we were to examine his conduct by the sober rules of philosophy and moral rectitude.

Andre's Letter *to General* Washington *has been thus beautifully paraphrased in verse by* N. P. Willis:

    "It is not the fear of death
        That damps my brow—
    It is not for another breath
        I ask thee now:
    I can die with a lip unstirred
        And a quiet heart,
    Let but this prayer be heard
        Ere I depart.

    "I can give up my mother's look,
        My sister's kiss,
    I can think of love—yet brook
        A death like this!
    I can give up the young fame
        I burned to win,
    All—but the spotless name
        I glory in.

"Thine is the power to give,
　Thine to deny,
Joy for the hour I live,
　Calmness to die:
By all the brave should cherish,
　By my dying breath,
I ask that I may perish
　By a soldier's death."

ARNOLD.

WE will cast a single glance on the dark path of Arnold after he had betrayed his country.

He fled from his post, and took refuge under the flag he had so long fought against. Anxious to distinguish himself in the field, and wipe out the deep stain upon his name, he solicited and obtained a command in Virginia; but two men were sent by the British General to watch him!

His Virginia expedition failed. He projected another: it was against his birthplace —his early neighbors and associates. It was to plunder the public stores of New London, feebly defended by Forts Griswold and Trumbull, at the mouth of the Thames.

Landing from Long Island, he sent a division of his troops against Fort Griswold: they took it, and entered New London. The town was reduced to ashes; vessels were burned; the brave Colonel Ledyard was slain with his own sword, after he had surrendered, and his companions butchered in cold blood. Now was the hour for the Traitor to complete his life of infamy! While the town where he used to play in his boyhood was burning, he stood in the belfry of a church of God, and looked exultingly on the conflagration!

This was the last exploit of the Traitor in his native land. He could henceforth live only in the nation whose gold had paid him for his treachery. He sailed for England. He entered London with a letter of introduction from Sir Henry Clinton to Lord George Germain.

When the petition for a bill authorizing peace with America was presented to the King by Parliament, the *Traitor* was standing near the throne, "apparently in high favor with his Majesty. Lord Lauderdale is reported to have declared, on returning to the House, ' that, however gracious might be the language he had heard from the throne, his indignation could not but be highly excited at beholding his Majesty supported by a Traitor.'" But his lordship should have found no fault with this spectacle. It was a *tableau* befitting the occasion: where else should the man who had betrayed the Republic find shelter, if not under the sceptre of a King whose gold had paid him for his villain work? It was, in fact, the *only* spot where the wretch could stand in security.

Lord Surrey, on another occasion, rose to speak in Parliament. Glancing his eye round the gallery, he saw Arnold; pointing towards him the finger of scorn, he exclaimed: "I will not speak while that man is in the House."

Arnold possessed, undoubtedly, animal courage: he could stand before a battery, and call on his men to advance. He was once at a levee in England immediately after the close of the American war, when he was introduced to Lord Balcarras as the American General, Arnold. "What! the *Traitor* Arnold?" exclaimed his lordship, turning on his heel with disgust. A challenge was given by the gen-

eral, and accepted by his lordship, who received Arnold's fire and discharged his own pistol in the air. "Why do you not return the fire?" exclaimed the General. "Because I am not an executioner," replied the nobleman, folding his arms, and looking disdainfully over his shoulder at his antagonist, as he quietly walked away from him.

The mark of Cain was on the brow of the Traitor, and he carried it to the grave. Wherever he went men read it. In England, in St. John's, in Guadaloupe—all through his restless, wandering life, it followed him still. He lived to see the young Republic he had betrayed emerge from the gloom of her long struggle into wealth, power, and splendor; and left it advancing on to empire as he went darkling down to a Traitor's grave!

He died in 1801, somewhere in the endless wilderness of London. Where he was buried we cannot tell. He died full of crime; and his name is covered with infamy by the execration of the nation he betrayed, and the nation which paid him for his traitor's work.

The following Acrostic, cut from a London paper of 1782, *is without exception one of the most severe comments ever passed upon the character of any man:*

ACROSTIC ON ARNOLD.

" Born for a curse to nature and mankind,
Earth's broadest realms can't show so black a mind;
Night's sable veil your crimes can never hide,
Each one so great would glut *historic* tide;
Defunct, your cursed memory will live
In all the glare that infamy can give;
Curses of ages will attend your name;
Traitors will glory in your shame.

"Almighty vengeance earnestly waits to roll
Rivers of sulphur on your treacherous soul;
Nature looks down, with conscious error sad,
On such a tarnished blot as she has made.
Let hell receive you, rivetted in chains,
Doomed to the hottest of its flames."
                              AMERICAN.

EXECUTION OF ANDRE.

Dr. Thatcher *makes this entry in his Journal on the Day of the Execution:*

"OCT. 2d. Major Andre is no more among the living. I have just witnessed his exit. It was a tragical scene of the deepest interest. * * * * The principal guard-officer, who was constantly in the room with the prisoner, relates that when the hour of his execution was announced to him in the morning, he received it without emotion, and, while all present were affected with silent gloom, he retained a firm countenance, with calmness and composure of mind. Observing his servant enter the room in tears, he exclaimed: 'Leave me until you can show yourself more

manly!' His breakfast being sent to him
from the table of General Washington, which
had been done every day of his confinement,
he partook of it as usual, and, having shaved
and dressed himself, he placed his hat on the
table, and cheerfully said to the guard-officers,
'I am ready at any moment, gentlemen, to
wait on you.' The fatal hour having arrived,
a large detachment of troops was paraded,
and an immense concourse of people assem-
bled; almost all our general and field officers,
except his Excellency and his staff, were present on horseback; melancholy and gloom per-
vaded all ranks, and the scene was affectingly
awful. I was so near, during the solemn
march to the fatal spot, as to observe every
movement, and participate in every emotion
which the melancholy scene was calculated to
produce. Major Andre walked from the stone
house in which he had been confined between
two of our subaltern officers arm-in-arm; the
eyes of the immense multitude were fixed on
him, who, rising superior to the fears of
death, appeared as if conscious of the digni-
fied deportment which he displayed. He betrayed no want of fortitude, but retained a

complacent smile on his countenance, and
politely bowed to several gentlemen whom he
knew, which was respectfully returned. It
was his earnest desire to be shot, as being
the mode of death most conformable to the
feelings of a military man, and he had indulged the hope that his request would be
granted. At the moment, therefore, when,
suddenly, he came in view of the gallows, he
involuntarily started backward, and made a
pause. 'Why this emotion, Sir?' said an
officer by his side. Instantly recovering his
composure, he said: 'I am reconciled to my
death, but I detest the mode!' While waiting, and standing near the gallows, I observed
some degree of trepidation: placing his foot
on a stone, and rolling it over, and choking
in his throat, as if attempting to swallow.
So soon, however, as he perceived things were
in readiness, he stepped quickly into the
wagon, and at this moment he appeared to
shrink, but instantly elevating his head with
firmness he said, 'It will be but a momentary
pang;' and taking from his pocket two white
handkerchiefs, the provost-marshal with one
loosely pinioned his arms, and with the other

the victim, after taking off his hat and stock, bandaged his own eyes with perfect firmness, which melted the hearts and moistened the cheeks not only of his servant but of the throng of spectators. The rope being appended to the gallows, he slipped the noose over his head, and adjusted it to his neck, without the assistance of the awkward executioner. Colonel Scammell now informed him that he had an opportunity to speak, if he desired it: he raised the handkerchief from his eyes, and said: 'I pray you to bear me witness that I meet my fate like a brave man.' The wagon being now removed from under him, he was suspended and instantly expired: it proved indeed but a momentary pang." (*Military Journal during the Revolutionary War*, by JAMES THATCHER, M.D., *Surgeon in the American Army*, 274.)

Major BENJAMIN RUSSELL *writes:*

"IT happened to be my turn, as a soldier of the Massachusetts line, to be on duty on the occasion, and to be posted in a situation where I could distinctly observe every part of the deportment of the gallant sufferer, and hear every word he uttered. He was dressed in the rich uniform of a British staff officer, with the exception, of course, of sash, gorget, sword, and spurs. * * * * The lofty gibbet was surrounded by an exterior guard of nearly five hundred infantry, with an inner guard of a captain's command. None were admitted within the square but the officers on duty and the assistants of the provost-marshal. The spectators outside the square were very numerous. Proceeding to the place of execution under the above guard, Andre was accompanied by two of the officers of the inner guard, which he had at first, as I learned, thought had been detailed as his executioners. He had previously requested of General Washington the favour of dying the death of a soldier. This mode of death the high sense of duty of the Commander-in-chief could not grant, and his delicacy forbade him to announce his determination in an answer. The officers of the American army performing duty on horseback, with General Greene at their head, were formed in line, on the road. To those whom Major Andre knew, particularly those who made part of the Board of General Officers who pronounced on his fate, he paid the salute of the hat, and received the adieus of all, with ease and complacency. The Commander-in-chief and staff were not present at the execution; and this mark of decorum, I was told, was feelingly appreciated by the sufferer. When the procession moved on the main road the gallows were not visible, but when it wheeled at an angle, the place of execution was seen directly in front. On viewing it the sufferer made a halt, and exhibited emotion. To an inquiry made by the guard, Major Andre gave the answer: 'I am reconciled to my death, but I detest the mode of it.' The Captain rejoined: 'It is unavoidable, Sir.' Arrived at the scaffold, Andre, after a short conversation with his servant, (who arrested much attention by the vehemence of his grief and loud lamentation,) ascended with gaiety the baggage-wagon. The general order of execution was then read by, I believe, Colonel Scammell. The reading was very impressive; and at the conclusion Major Andre uncovered, bowed to the General and other officers, and said, with dignity and firmness, 'All I request of you, gentlemen, is that you will bear witness to the world that I die like a brave man.' He added nothing more aloud, but while the preparations for immediate execution were being made, he said, in an undertone, 'It will be but a momentary pang.' Thus died Major John Andre, Adjutant-General to the British army. The sympathy of the American officers was universally expressed, and the Father of our Country, in announcing his death to Congress, pronounced that he met his fate like a brave man." (*New England Magazine*, vi. 363.)

Major TALLMADGE *writes, in a letter to a friend:*

"POOR Andre, who has been under my charge almost ever since he was taken, has yesterday had his trial, and though his sentence is not known, a disgraceful death is no doubt allotted to him. By heavens! Colonel Webb, I never saw a man whose fate I foresaw whom I so sincerely pitied. He is a young fellow of the greatest accomplishments, and was the prime minister of Sir Harry on all occasions. He has unbosomed his heart to me so fully, and indeed let me know almost every motive of his actions since he came out on his late mission, and he has endeared me to him exceedingly. Unfortunate man! He will undoubtedly suffer death to-morrow, and though he knows his fate, seems to be as cheerful as though he were going to an assembly. I am sure he will go to the gallows less fearful for his fate, and with less concern than I shall behold the tragedy. Had he been tried by a court of ladies, he is so genteel, handsome, polite a young gentleman, that I am confident they would have acquitted him.

But enough of Andre, who, though he dies lamented, falls justly."

The same officer, in other communications upon the subject, says:

"From the moment that Andre made the disclosure of his name and true character, in his letter to the Commander-in-chief, which he handed to me as soon as he had written it, down to the moment of his execution, I was almost constantly with him. I walked with him to the place of execution, and parted with him under the gallows, overwhelmed with grief that so gallant an officer and so accomplished a gentleman should come to such an ignominious end. The ease and affability of his manners, polished by the refinement of good society, and a finished education, made him a most delightful companion. It often drew tears from my eyes to find him so agreeable in conversation on different subjects, when I reflected on his future fate, and that, too, as I believed, so near at hand."

"When he came within sight of the gibbet, he appeared to be startled, and inquired with some emotion whether he was not to be shot. Being informed that the mode first appointed for his death could not consistently be altered, he exclaimed, 'How hard is my fate!' but immediately added, 'It will soon be over!' I then shook hands with him under the gallows and retired." (*Spark's Arnold*, 255; *Irving's Washington*, iv. 149, 157.)

NAMES
OF THE
SUBSCRIBERS TO THE FOLIO COPIES
OF
ANDREANA.

No.				
1.	JOHN CAMPBELL,	10 copies.	Philadelphia.
11.	C. B. RICHARDSON,	4 "	New York.
15.	T. H. MORRELL,	2 "	"
17.	FRANCIS S. HOFFMAN,		"
18.	RICHARD W. ROCHE,		"
19.	JOHN SABIN,		"
20.	FRANCIS B. HAYES,		"
21.	W. ELLIOTT WOODWARD,		Roxbury, Mass.
22.	HENRY A. SMITH,		Cleveland, Ohio.
23.	WILLIAM A. WHITEMAN,		Philadelphia.
24.	WILLIAM W. LONG,		"
25.	HORACE W. SMITH,		"

NAMES

OF THE

SUBSCRIBERS TO THE QUARTO COPIES

OF

ANDREANA.

No.				
1.	JOHN CAMPBELL,	10 copies.	PHILADELPHIA.
11.	C. B. RICHARDSON,	6 "	NEW YORK.
17.	T. H. MORRELL,	5 "	"
22.	C. A. MILLER,	2 "	"
24.	J. W. BOUTON,	3 "	"
27.	W. ELLIOTT WOODWARD,		ROXBURY, MASS.
28.	FRANCIS S. HOFFMAN,		NEW YORK.
29.	WINTHROP SARGENT, N.Y. PER J. PENNINGTON & SON.
30.	S. M. L. BARLOW,	"	"
31.	CHARLES J. BUSHNELL, "		"
32.	FREEMAN M. JOSSELYN, BOSTON,		"

SUBSCRIBERS.

No. 33.	GEORGE CLASBACK,	New York,	Per G. French.
34.	G. H. MATHEWS,	"	"
35.	S. S. PURPLE, M.D.,	"	"
36.	CHARLES CONGDON,	"	"
37.	A. W. GRISWOLD,	"	"
38.	JOHN F. McCOY,	"	"
39.	E. FRENCH, 4 copies.	"	"
43.	JOHN P. DESFORGES,	Baltimore, Md.	
44.	A. C. KLINE,	Philadelphia.	
45.	SIMON GRATZ,	"	
46.	JOHN A. McALLASTER,	"	
47.	WILLIAM B. MANN,	"	
48.	JOHN SABIN,	New York.	
49.	ELIAS DEXTER,	"	
50.	NATHAN S. PETERSON,	Philadelphia.	

No. _____

Edition of 175 *Copies,*
Of which 25 *are in Folio,*
50 *in Quarto,*
and 100 *in* 8vo.

CENTENNIAL OF THE CAPTURE

OF

MAJOR ANDRÉ.

ORATION AT TARRYTOWN,

THURSDAY, SEPTEMBER 23d, 1880.

BY

Hon. CHAUNCEY M. DEPEW.

NEW YORK:
JOHN POLHEMUS, PRINTER, 102 NASSAU STREET.
1880.

CENTENNIAL OF THE CAPTURE

OF

MAJOR ANDRÉ.

Oration at Tarrytown,

SEPTEMBER 23d, 1880.

Hon. CHAUNCEY M. DEPEW.

NEW YORK:
JOHN POLHEMUS, PRINTER, 102 NASSAU STREET.

1880.

CENTENNIAL OF THE CAPTURE

OF

MAJOR ANDRÉ.

One hundred years ago the sun rose upon the same beautiful landscape which surrounds us here to-day. The noble Hudson rolled in front; to the north were the Highlands, in their majesty and strength; on the west towered the mountains enclosing the Bay, and on the east spread valleys and hills celebrated then, as now, for their picturesqueness and commanding views. Beyond the loveliness of the situation it had no greater claims upon the attention of the world than hundreds of places adorned by nature which have made our State celebrated for the beauty and variety of its scenery. But when the sun went down this spot had become one of the fields priceless in the memory of mankind, where virtue is vindicated, and civilization and liberty saved from great disaster. The story we repeat here has as much value as a lesson to the living as a reverent tribute to the memory of the dead.

History, traditions, legends forgotten, almost lost, in the rapid march of events, and the wonderful development of material prosperity, are so revived by these commemorations that our county, richer than any other in the commonwealth in revolutionary recollections, becomes in every part a perpetual teacher of the labors and sacrifices of patriotism to secure our independence.

The happiness and progress of mankind have as often been advanced or retarded by small events as by great battles. If the three hundred men with Leonidas stemmed the Persian torrent, and made Thermopylæ the inspiration of twenty centuries, right here a century ago to-day three plain farmers of Westchester preserved the liberties of the American people.

It is hard, even in imagination, to understand now the condition of this region at that period. It was ominously known as the neutral ground, and marauded and harried by Royal and Continental soldiers, and by Skinners and Cow-boys, robbers and brigands of equal infamy. The Whig farmer saw his cattle driven off and the flames of his buildings lighting the sky to-night, and mercilessly retaliated upon his Tory neighbor to-morrow. Fences were down, fruit rotted ungathered on the ground, rank vegetation covered the unsown fields, and the gaunt and vengeful citizen guarded with ready musket his family and hidden stores, or watched in ambuscade by the wayside to recapture his stolen property or prevent the delivery of foraged stores to the enemy. Amidst such experiences and surroundings the captors of André passed their daily lives.

September, 1780, was a gloomy and anxious time for Washington and Congress. Charleston had fallen, and Gates had been disastrously defeated. With the rout of his army the whole South had come under the enemy's control. New Jersey was overrun, and twenty thousand men, veterans of European battle-fields, were gathered in New York. The French fleet had sailed away, and a large reinforcement arrived to the British navy, and Washington's cherished plan of a demonstration against the city had to be abandoned. The only American force worthy the name of an army, numbering less than twelve thousand, suffering from long arrears of pay, without money to send their starving families, and short of every kind of supplies, was encamped at and about West Point. This critical moment was selected by Arnold, with devilish sagacity, to strike his deadly blow. Elated by the successes which had crowned his earlier efforts, he plunged into excesses, which left him without a command, bankrupt in fortune, and smarting under the reprimand of Congress. He still retained the confidence of Washington, and anxious to secure the largest price for his treason applied for and obtained the command of West Point.

The surrender of this post, controlling the passes of the Hudson, with its war materials vital to the maintainance of the patriot army, and its garrison of four thousand troops, together with the person of Washington, ended, in his judgment, the war, and gave him a place second to Monk in English history.

The success or failure of the united colonies in forming an independent government depended, from the beginning to the end of the contest, on the State of New York.

Through her boundaries ran the natural channels by which the Six Nations marched to Savage Empire; the English broke the French power on this continent, and emigration and commerce have peopled and enriched great states. A British statesman and soldier said: "Fortify from Canada to the City of New York, and we can hold the colonies together." The British Cabinet and Generals said: "Capture and place a chain of posts along the route from New York City to Canada, and we can crush rebellious New England and awe all the rest into submission." The battle of Saratoga and surrender of Burgoyne defeated the last and most formidable attempt to accomplish this result by arms. Upon its bloody field American Independence was consummated. That grand victory which gave us unity at home and recognition abroad was largely due to the skill, the dash, the intrepid valor of Arnold.

The issue decided in that conflict the control of the passes of the Hudson, and all which would follow was now to be reopened and reversed by treason, and the traitor the same Arnold. For eighteen months a correspondence opened by Arnold had been carried on between him and Major André, acting for Sir Henry Clinton.

He wrote over the signature of Gustavus, seeking a bid for his defection, and occasionally imparting valuable information to indicate his importance. André replied under the name of John Anderson, testing and tempting.

These letters, moulded in the vocabulary of trade, and treating of the barter and sale of cattle and goods, were really haggling about the price of the betrayal of the liberties of America and a human soul. The time had come for action, and the British must be satisfied as to the identity of their man and the firmness of his purpose, and commit him beyond the possibility of retreat. For said Sir Henry Clinton, "We propose to risk no lives upon the possibilities of deceit or failure." The first meeting appointed at Dobbs Ferry, on the 12th of September, failed, and Arnold came near being captured. With rare audacity he reported his visit at once to Washington, and the next day wrote a letter to General Greene expressing bitter indignation against Gates for his Southern defeat, and the apprehension that it would leave an indelible stain upon his reputation.

Armed with a decoy letter from Beverly Robinson, ostensibly about his confiscated lands, really conveying information where an interview with André might be had, he met Washington, on his way to see Rochambeau at Hartford, carried him across the river at Verplancks Point in his barge, and asked permission to go, but the chief declined, saying the matter had better be left to the civil authorities. An overruling Providence was protecting the patriot cause and weaving about the plot the elements of its exposure and destruction. Baffled, but not disheartened, Arnold, lurking in the bushes of the Long Clove below Haverstraw, sent a boat at midnight to the Vulture to bring André to the shore. The boatmen, roughly handled on the sloop of war for daring to approach her without a flag of truce, are hurried before André and explain their mission. He disguised his uniform in a cloak and determined to accompany them. The caution of Sir Henry Clinton—not to go within the American lines, not to cover his uniform, not to be the bearer of any papers—rings in his ears. The warning hand of Beverly Robinson rests upon his shoulder. The danger, the disgrace, the prize, are before him. If detected, a spy; if successful, at the head of a victorious column upon Fort Putnam receiving the surrender of West Point: a General's Commission; the thanks of Parliament; the knightly honors of his King. Brilliant, accomplished, captivating, chivalric and ambitious, his secret correspondence had revealed the defect in his character; his moral sense was paralyzed in the presence of great opportunities.

The dawn finds Arnold and André still in the thicket, still disputing about the terms. Horses are hastily mounted and they start for Smith's House, still standing yonder above the bay.

The sentinel's challenge, the countersign, warn André that he is in the last position of a soldier : disguised and on a secret mission within the enemy's camp. All the morning that fearful bargaining goes on, and at last it is settled. He receives the papers giving the plans, fortifications, armament and troops at West Point, the proceedings of Washington's last council of war, and hides them between his stockings and his feet. He receives the assurance that the defences shall be so manned as to fall without a blow, and assures Arnold in return of a Brigadier-Generalship in the British army, and seven thousand pounds in money, and bids him farewell, till he meets him at the close of a sham combat to receive his surrender and sword.

Those two men thus bidding adieu on yonder hillside have determined the destinies of unborn millions, and none share their secret, and there is no one to betray them. Once safely back with those papers, and America's doom is sealed. We bow with devout and humble thanksgiving to the watchful and beneficent Providence which turned most trivial circumstances into the powerful elements which thwarted this well-laid scheme. Colonel Livingston, commanding at Verplancks, refused by Arnold a heavy gun to fire upon the Vulture, had made it so hot for her with a little four-pounder on Teller's Point, that she had dropped down the river. The timid Smith, of whom posterity is in doubt whether he was a knave or a tool, was too scared to venture to reach her by boat, and so the land journey was determined upon. Still further disguised, and armed with Arnold's pass in the name of John Anderson, André crossed the river on the afternoon of the 22d of September to Verplancks Point, and safely passed through Livingston's camp.

Gaily he rides, accompanied by Smith, through the Cortlandt woods, and over the Yorktown hills. He laughs as he passes the ancient guide-post, bearing its legend, "*Dishe his di Roode toe de Kshings Farray,*" and his hair stood on end, he said, when he met Colonel Webb, of our army, whom he perfectly knew, but who stared and went on. His plan is to strike the White Plains road and so reach his own lines. But at Crumpond, Captain Boyd stops them. A most uncomfortable, inquisitive, vigilant, and troublesome Yankee, is this same Captain Boyd. Arnold's pass stuns him, but it requires all the versatility and adroitness of André to allay his suspicions. He so significantly recommends their remaining all night that they dare not decline. A Westchester farmer's bed never had two more uneasy occupants.

At early dawn they departed, with Captain Boyd in the rear, and the Cow-boys, against whom Boyd had warned them, in front—André's spirits rose. He had left disgrace and a shameful death behind, and saw only escape, glory and renown before. Hitherto taciturn and depressed, he now overwhelmed his dazed companions with a flood of brilliant talk.

Poetry, music, belles lettres, the drama, the times, formed the theme of his flowing eloquence, and ever and anon as they rose the many eminences which command a view of the Highlands, and the river, he broke out in rapturous praise of the entrancing scenery. Mrs. Underhill, near Pine's Bridge, had lost her all, but one cow and a bag of meal, by a raid of the Cow-boys the night before, but with true county hospitality she spread before them the time-honored Westchester dish of suppawn and milk. At Pine's Bridge, Smith's courage failed and he bade his companion good-bye. This was another of the trivial incidents which led André to his fate. Smith, with his acquaintance and ready wit, would have piloted him safely by the White Plains road, or upon the other route, and satisfied the scruples of the yeomen who captured him. Smith rode to West Point and by his report allayed Arnold's anxiety, and then in the easy and shiftless character of everybody's friend he continued on to Fishkill and supped with Washington and his staff. André alone, free from care, decided to strike for the river—it was a shorter road—and from the Cow-boys who infested it he had nothing to fear; but it was another link in the chain winding about him. The broad domains of his friends, the great loyalist families, lay about him, his own lines a few short hours beyond.

Saturday morning, the 23d of September, one hundred years ago, was one of those clear, bright, exhilarating days, when this region is in the fullness of its quiet beauty. The handsome horseman delights the children of Staats Hammond's family as they hand him a cup of water, and leaves a lasting impression upon the Quakers of Chappaqua, of whom he inquires the distance to Tarrytown. Through Sparta, he strikes the river road, and gallops along that most picturesque highway, the scenery in harmony with the brilliant future spread before his imagination. He recognizes the old Sleepy Hollow Church, with its ancient bell bearing the motto, *Si Deus pro nobis, quis contra nos*, and a half mile in front sees the bridge over the little brook which was to be for him a fatal Rubicon On the south side of that stream, in the bushes playing cards, were three young farmers of the neighborhood—John Paulding, David Williams and Isaac Van Wart—watching to intercept the Cow-boys and their stolen cattle. At the approach of the horseman, Paulding steps into the road, presents his musket and calls a halt. It was nine in the morning; they have been there but an hour. An earlier start, a swifter pace, and André would have escaped; but this was still another of the trivial incidents in the fatal combination about him André speaks first. "My lads, I hope you belong to our party." "Which party," they said. "The lower party," he answered. "We do." "Then thank God," said he, "I am once more among friends. I am a British officer, out on particular business, and must not be detained a minute." Then they said, "We are Americans, and you are our prisoner and must dismount." "My God," he said, laughing, "a man must do anything to get along," and presented Arnold's pass. Had he presented it first, Paulding said, afterwards, he would have let him go. They carefully scanned it, but persisted in detaining him. He threatened them with Arnold's vengeance for this disrespect to his order; but, in language more forcible than polite, they told him "they cared not for that," and led him to the great whitewood tree, under which he was searched. As the fatal papers fell from his feet, Paulding said, "My God, here it is," and, as he read them, shouted in high excitement to his companions, "By God, he is a spy."

Now came the crucial and critical moment. André, fully alive to his danger, and with every faculty alert, felt no alarm. He had, the day before bargained with and successfully bought an American Major-General of the highest military reputation.

If a few thousand pounds and a commission in the British army could seduce the commander of a district, surely escape was easy from these three young men, but one of whom could read, and who were buttressed by neither fame nor fortune. "If you will release me," said André, "I will give you a hundred guineas and any amount of dry goods." "I will give you a thousand guineas," he cried, "and you can hold me hostage till one of your number returns with the money."

Then Paulding swore, "We would not let you go for

ten thousand guineas." That decision saved the liberties of America. It voiced the spirit which sustained and carried through the revolutionary struggle for nationality, and crushed the rebellion waged eighty years afterwards to destroy that nationality—the invincible courage and impregnable virtue of the common people.

As Washington was riding that night from Hartford, depressed by the refusal of Count Rochambeau, the French General, to co-operate in his plans, and to be overwhelmed on the morrow by Arnold's astounding treason, all along the route enthusiastic throngs with torches and acclamations hailed his approach. "We may be beaten by the English," he said to Rochambeau's Aid, "it is the fortune of war; but behold an army which they can never conquer."

With one of his captors in front, the others on either side of his horse, André is carried to Colonel Jameson's, the nearest American post. The gay horseman has come to grief, and the buoyant gallop to the front has turned into a funeral march to the rear, and he recalls the ill omen of the song sung by Wolfe the night before the storming of Quebec, and which he had repeated at the farewell dinner given him the evening of his departure on this fatal errand.

> Why, soldiers, why,
> Should we be melancholy boys,
> Why, soldiers, why,
> Whose business 'tis to die.

Jameson, a brave and honest soldier, was easily duped

by the courtly arts of André. While he sent the papers by special messenger to Washington, he was persuaded by André to forward him with a letter descriptive of his capture to Arnold. Once there and both had escaped. The vigilant and suspicious Major Tallmadge induced Jameson to bring back André; but to recall the letter to Arnold, he positively refused. Jameson's messenger to Washington, mistaking his road, did not reach West Point till the next noon; his messenger to Arnold arrived in the morning.

Washington, on approaching the river, according to his habit, proceeded at once to examine the fortifications. La Fayette reminded him that Mrs. Arnold's breakfast was waiting. "You young gentleman are all in love with Mrs. Arnold," he said. "You go and tell her not to wait for me, I will be there in a short time." Hamilton and McHenry delivered the message, and were welcomed by Arnold and his wife.

In the midst of the meal Allan, the messenger, delivered Jameson's letter. Arnold's iron nerve held him unconcernedly at the table a few moments; then, saying he must go over to the Point to prepare for the reception of the General, he arose.

His wife followed him up stairs. Hastily informing her of his ruin and bidding her perhaps a last farewell, as she fell fainting to the floor, he kissed his sleeping baby, stepped a moment into the breakfast room to inform his guests of the sudden illness of his wife, and, followed by his boat's crew, dashed down the hillside to the river.

They must row with all their might, he told them, as he had a message to deliver on board the Vulture, eighteen miles below, for Washington, and should be back before evening. He reprimed his pistols, and, with one in each hand, sat resolved to die the death of a suicide rather than be captured. By promises of reward, by voice and gesture, he urges his crew to their best exertions. His guilty soul peopling every turn of the river with avenging pursuit, he sails through the Highlands, waving his handkerchief as a flag to his forts, redoubts and patrols, astonishing the vigilant Livingston at Verplancks with the spectacle of his commander making straight for the British sloop of war, and takes the first free breath of relief as he steps on the deck of the Vulture.

To his coxswain he offers a commission, to the crew rewards, if they will desert and join the British. They unanimously refuse, and Larvey the coxswain replies: "If General Arnold likes the King of England, let him serve him; we love our country, and intend to live or die in support of her cause." At Arnold's command they are made prisoners, and he stood there among them then, as he stands pilloried in history for all time, the only American soldier who, during the revolutionary war, turned traitor to his country. As Washington returns from the inspection at West Point, to Arnold's headquarters, at the Robinson

House, he finds Hamilton, holding Jameson's letters and the papers found on André. Then he understands Arnold's sudden flight, the failure to greet him from the batteries with the accustomed salute, the general negligence and want of preparation for attack everywhere found He stands on a mine. How far does this conspiracy extend? Who else are implicated? The enemy may come this very night, and who shall be placed in posts of danger? Despairingly he says : " Whom can we trust now?"

But Washington's greatness shone conspicuously in great emergencies. Hamilton is dispatched to intercept Arnold, if possible, Tallmadge is ordered to bring André with triple guards to West Point, Greene at Tappan is directed to put the whole army in marching order, and before night every fort and defence from Putnam to Verplancks is ready for any assault. Then, with no outward sign of excitement, Washington sat down to dinner, and with courtly kindness sent word to Arnold's hysterical and screaming wife : "It was my duty to arrest General Arnold, and I have used every exertion to do so, but I take pleasure in informing *you* that he is now safe on board the Vulture." André was brought to West Point that night, and taken to the headquarters of the army at Tappan the next day. According to the laws and usages of war in relation to spies, Washington could have ordered him summarily to execution. But threats of retaliation, impudent letters from Arnold, extraordinary appeals and interpretations of André's conduct and position from Sir Henry Clinton, began to pour in upon the Commander-in-Chief. He ordered a board of officers to be convened, and submitted the case to their consideration. It was as august a tribunal as ever sat under like circumstances: six major-generals and eight brigadiers—as eminent as any in the service, including the foreign officers La Fayette and Steuben—formed the Court. They gave André every opportunity to present his own defence, and when the facts were all in, unanimously adjudged him guilty, and that he must suffer the death of a spy. His youth, graces and accomplishments, his dignity and cheerfulness, won the affections of his guard and the tenderest sympathy of the whole army. There was not a soldier present who would not have risked his life, if by so doing Arnold might be captured and substituted in André's place. In all the glittering splendor of the full uniform and ornaments of his rank, in the presence of the whole American army, without the quiver of a muscle or sign of fear, the officers about him weeping, the bands playing the dead march, he walked to execution. His last words were of loving solicitude for the welfare of mother and sisters in distant Britain, and the manner of fame he would leave behind. "How hard is my fate, but it will be but a momentary pang," he said, as he pushed aside the executioner and himself adjusted the rope. To those around he cried: "I pray you to bear witness that I meet my fate like a brave man," and swung into eternity.

The supernatural served to add to the interest and perpetuate the memory of this tragedy. On the day of his execution the great tree under which he was searched was shattered by a bolt of lightning; and at the same hour, at his home in England, his sister awoke from a troubled sleep screaming, "My brother is dead; he has been hung as a spy."

In the British Army, and in England, the wildest indignation burst out against Washington. André was mourned and honored as if he had fallen in a moment of glorious victory at the head of his column. His brother was knighted, his family pensioned, and his King declared in solemn message that "the public can never be compensated for the vast advantages which must have followed from the success of his plan." In Westminster Abbey, that grand mausoleum of England's mighty dead, where repose her greatest statesmen, warriors and authors, the King placed a monument bearing this inscription: "Sacred to the memory of Major John André, who, raised by his merit, at an early period of his life, to the rank of Adjutant-General of the British forces in America, and employed in an important but hazardous enterprise, fell a sacrifice to his zeal for his King and country."

Forty years afterwards a Royal embassy came to this country, disinterred his remains at Tappan, and a British frigate sent for the purpose bore them to England, where they were buried beside his monument with imposing ceremonies. One of the most enlightened and liberal of England's churchmen, in a recent visit to this land, wrote the inscription for, and urged the erection of, the monument to André's memory at Tappan, as the one act which would do more than anything else to remove the last vestiges of enmity between the United States and Great Britain.

André's story is the one overmastering romance of the revolution. American and English literature are full of eloquence and poetry in tribute to his memory and sympathy for his fate. After the lapse of a hundred years there is no abatement of absorbing interest. What had this young man done to merit immortality? The mission, whose tragic issue lifted him out of the oblivion of other minor British officers, in its inception was free from peril or daring, and its objects and purposes were utterly infamous. Had he succeeded by the desecration of the honorable uses of passes and flags of truce, his name would have been held in everlasting execration. In his failure, the infant Republic escaped the dagger with which he was feeling for its heart, and the crime was drowned in tears for his untimely end. His youth and beauty, his skill with pen and pencil, his effervescing spirits and magnetic disposition, the brightness of his life, the calm courage in the gloom of his death, his early love and disappointment, and the image of his lost Honora hid in his mouth when captured in Canada, with the exclamation, "That saved, I care not for the loss of all the rest," and nestling in his bosom when he was slain, surrounded him with a halo of poetry and pity which have secured for him what he most sought and could never have won in battles and sieges—a fame and recognition which have outlived that of all the generals under whom he served.

Are Kings only grateful, and do Republics forget? Is

fame a travesty, and the judgment of mankind a farce? America had a parallel case in Captain Nathan Hale. Of the same age as André, he graduated at Yale College with high honors, enlisted in the patriot cause at the beginning of the contest, and secured the love and confidence of all about him. When none else would go upon a most important and perilous mission, he volunteered, and was captured by the British. While André received every kindness, courtesy and attention, and was fed from Washington's table, Hale was thrust into a noisome dungeon in the sugar-house. While André was tried by a board of officers, and had ample time and every facility for defence, Hale was summarily ordered to execution the next morning. While André's last wishes and bequests were sacredly followed, the infamous Cunningham tore from Hale his cherished Bible, and destroyed before his eyes his last letters to his mother and sister, and asked him what he had to say. "All I have to say," was Hale's reply, "I regret I have but one life to lose for my country." His death was concealed for months, because Cunningham said he did not want the rebels to know they had a man who could die so bravely. And yet, while André rests in that grandest of mausoleums, where the proudest of nations garners the remains and perpetuates the memories of its most eminent and honored children, the name and deeds of Nathan Hale have passed into oblivion, and only a simple tomb in a village church-yard marks his resting-place. The dying declarations of André and Hale express the animating spirit of their several armies, and teach why, with all her power, England could not conquer America. "I call upon you to witness that I die like a brave man," said André, and he spoke from British and Hessian surroundings, seeking only glory and pay. "I regret I have but one life to lose for my country," said Hale; and with him and his comrades self was forgotten in that absorbing, passionate patriotism which pledges fortune, honor and life to the sacred cause.

But Republics are not ungrateful. The captors of André were honored and rewarded in their lives, and grateful generations celebrate their deeds and revere their memories. Washington wrote to Congress: "The party that took Major André acted in such a manner as does them the highest honor, and proves them to be men of great virtue ; their conduct gives them a just claim to the thanks of their country." Congress acted promptly. It thanked them by resolution, granted to each an annuity of two hundred dollars for life, and twelve hundred and fifty dollars in cash, or the same amount in confiscated lands in Westchester County, and directed a silver medal bearing the motto "Fidelity" on the one side and "Vincit Amor Patriæ" on the other, to be presented to them. The Legislature of the State of New York gave to each of them a farm in consideration—reads the act—of "their virtue in refusing a large sum offered to them by Major André as a bribe to permit him to escape." Shortly after, Washington gave a grand dinner party at

Verplancks Point. At the table were his staff and the famous generals of the army, and as honored guests these three young men—Paulding, Williams and Van Wart—whose names were now household words all over the land; and there with solemn and impressive speech Washington presented the medals. Paulding died in 1818, and in 1827 the Corporation of the City of New York placed a monument over his grave in the old cemetery just north of Peekskill, reciting, "The Corporation of the City of New York erected this Tomb as a Memorial Sacred to Public Gratitude," the Mayor delivering the address and a vast concourse participating in the ceremonies. Van Wart died in 1828, and in the Greenburgh church-yard the citizens of this county erected a memorial in "Testimony of his virtuous and patriotic conduct." Williams died in Livingstonville, in Schoharie County, in 1831, and was buried with military honors. In 1876 the State erected a monument, and his remains were re-interred in the old stone fort at Schoharie Court House. On the spot where André was captured the young men of Westchester County, in 1853, built a cenotaph in honor of his captors. Arnold, burned in effigy in every village and hamlet in America, received his money and a commission in the British army, but was daily insulted by the proud and honorable officers upon whom his association was forced, and who despised alike the treason and the traitor. His infamy has served to gild and gloss the acts of André, and deepening with succeeding years brings out with each generation a clearer and purer appreciation of the virtue and patriotism of Paulding, Williams and Van Wart.

Pity for André led to grave injustice to Washington and detraction of his captors, which a century has not effaced. Sir Henry Clinton and his officers, in addresses and memoirs, denounced the execution of André as without justification. A contemporary British poetess characterized Washington as a "remorseless murderer," and one of the latest and ablest of England's historians says this act is the one indelible "blot upon his character," and that the decision of the military tribunal composed of men ignorant of Vattel and Puffendorff, and fresh from "plough handles and shop boards," does not relieve him. It has become a conviction abroad, and to some extent a sentiment here, that a grave and fatal error was committed. It is claimed that André was under the protection of a flag of truce, that he was within the American lines upon the invitation of the commander of the district, and under the protection of that General's pass, that his intent was free from turpitude, and the circumstances surrounding his position entitled him to exchange or discharge. When André was on trial upon the charge of being a spy, he testified in his own behalf that "he had no reason to suppose he came on shore under a flag of truce," and such is the concurrent testimony of all the witnesses. The story was the subsequent invention of

Arnold. But even if true, the flag is recognized in the usages of war for definite and honorable purposes—it ameliorates the horrors of the conflict; but, when used as a cover for treasonable purposes, loses its character and protective power. To present it as a defence and shield for the corrupt correspondence of the enemy's emissary and a traitorous officer, is a monstrous perversion. It is true, he was present at Arnold's invitation and carried his pass, but he knew the object of his visit, and did not hold the pass in his own name and title. Months before he had written to Colonel Sheldon, commanding the Continental outposts, that under flag and pass he proposed visiting, on important business, General Arnold, at West Point, and requesting safe conduct, and signing and representing himself as John Anderson, a trader. The meeting which finally took place was an appointment often before thwarted, and its object to tamper with the integrity and seduce from his allegiance the enemy's officer. The signals and agencies of communication and travel between hostile forces were collusively used to procure the betrayal of an army and the ruin of a nation. André landed at Haverstraw to traffic with the necessities and tempt the irritated pride of a bankrupt and offended general, and having succeeded in seducing him to surrender the forts and trusts under his command, Benedict Arnold, so far as his confederate André was concerned, ceased from that moment to be the American commander, and any papers issued by him to further and conceal the scheme were absolutely void. His pass and safe conduct were not only vitiated in their inception by the joint act of giver and receiver, secreting treason in them, but they were issued to an assumed name and borne in a false character. A British soldier found disguised in the American lines, with the plans of the patriots' forts, the details of their armaments and the outlines of the plot for their betrayal hidden in his boots, lost, with the discovery of his personality and purposes, the protection of a fraudulent certificate. Greene and Knox, and La Fayette and Steuben, and the other members of the board of officers who tried and convicted André, may possibly have been ignorant of the great authorities upon international law; but had they studied, they would have found in them both precedent and justification. While the laws of war justify tampering with the opposing commander and compassing his desertion, the sudden, unsuspected, unguardable and overwhelming character of the blow render it the highest of crimes, and subjects those detected and arrested in the act to summary execution. A general is commissioned by his government to fight its battles and protect its interests. The law of principal and agent is as applicable as to a civil transaction, and all who deal with him, to betray his trust, know that he is acting beyond the limits of his authority. Not the least remarkable of the incidents of this strange history, was the proposition of Sir Henry Clinton to submit the question to the arbitration of the French General Rochambeau and the Hessian General Knyphausen. Such an offer would never have been made to a European commander. It was an expression in a form most offensive to Washington, of that supercilious contempt for the abilities, acquirements and opinions of American soldiers and statesmen, on the part of the ruling classes in England, which precipitated the Revolution and created this Republic. The sympathy and grief of Washington for André and his misfortunes were among the deepest and profoundest emotions of his life. The most urgent public necessity, the most solemn of public duties demanded his decision. The country and the army were dismayed by the plot, which Congress declared would have been ruinous to the cause, which Greene proclaimed in general order would have been a fatal stab at our liberties, which King George the Third said possessed advantages that, if successful, could not be estimated, and as Sir Henry Clinton wrote, would have ended the conflict. Washington's remark to La Fayette, "Whom can we trust now," echoed the sentiment of the hour. In that supreme moment private considerations and personal pity surrendered to the requirements of official responsibility, and General Washington, the Commander-in-chief, stamped out treasonable sentiment within, and deterred treasonable efforts without, by signing the death warrant of Major John André.

André left as a legacy a blow at his captors, which, thirty-seven years afterwards, bore extraordinary fruit. In 1817 one of them petitioned Congress for an increase of pension, and Major Tallmadge, then a member, assailed them with great vigor and virulence. He had been a distinguished officer in the Revolutionary war. It was by his energy and sagacity that Lt.-Col. Jameson was prevented delivering André to Arnold, and he was in command of the guard and with André till his death. Like all the young American officers about him, Tallmadge formed a warm friendship for him, and admiration of his character and accomplishments. He asserted that his captors were Cow-boys, and that it was André's opinion, frequently expressed, that they stopped him for plunder, and would have released him if he could have given security for his ransom. Tallmadge knew nothing of either of them prior to this event, and his judgment was wholly the reflex of André's expressions. André's remarks were either a deliberate stab at the reputations of the men towards whom the nation's gratitude was already rising with a volume which promised an immortality of fame, while he was waiting a shameful death, or in his dread extremity he could neither understand any higher motive in them to resist his offers, or regard with tolerance or patience these humble peasants whose acts had ruined his fortunes and delivered him to his fate. But against assertions and theories stand the impregnable facts of history. They did reject bribes beyond the wildest dreams of any wealth they ever hoped to accumulate. They did deliver him to the nearest American post, and neither asked or expected any reward. Van Wart had served four years in the Westchester Militia, and his term of enlistment had but recently expired. Paulding had been twice a British prisoner of war in New York, and was a third time wounded in their hands at the declaration of peace, and the Yager uniform in which he had escaped but four days before the capture misled André into the impulsive revelation of his rank. Security for the ransom they had. As they were intelligent enough to understand the importance of their prisoner, they knew that while two held him as hostage, the third could arrange for the delivery of any sum he promised upon his release.

Washington, the Continental Congress and the Legislature of our own State are the contemporary witnesses, and their testimonies by words and deeds are part of the record which makes this day memorable. When the news of Major Tallmadge's charges was received here, sixteen of the most respected and reputable men of our County, names as familiar among us as household words, certified to Congress, "that during the revolutionary war they were well acquainted with Isaac Van Wart, David Williams and John Paulding, and that at no time during the revolutionary war was any suspicion entertained by their neighbors or acquaintances that they or either of them held any undue intercourse with the enemy. On the contrary, they were universally esteemed, and taken to be ardent and faithful in the cause of the country." Van Wart and Paulding, in solemn affidavits, reasserted the details of the capture and the motives of their conduct. As each of them, in ripe old age and the fullness of years, was called to render his account to the Great Judge, mourning thousands gathered about the graves to testify their reverence; and the respect and gratitude of their countrymen reared monuments to their memories.

The population, prosperity, wealth and luxury which surround us here have grown upon the devastated fields of a century ago.

We rededicate this cenotaph in honor of those whose virtues made possible this result. The peace, civilization, liberty and happiness we enjoy at home, the power which commands for us respect abroad, lie in the strength and perpetuity of our Republican institutions. Had they been lost by battle or treason in the revolutionary struggle, or sunk in the bloody chasm of civil war, the grand nationality of to-day would have been dependent provinces, or warring and burdened States. Arnold and André, Paulding, Williams and Van Wart are characters in a drama which crystalizes an eternal principle, that these institutions rest upon the integrity and patriotism of the common people. We are not here to celebrate marches, sieges and battles. The trumpet, the charge, the waving plume, the flying enemy, the hero's death, are not our inspiration. The light which made clear to these men the priceless value of country and liberty was but the glimmering dawn, compared with the noonday glory of the full-orbed radiance in which we stand.

As a hundred years has ripened the fame and enriched the merit of their deed, so will it be rehearsed with increasing gratitude by each succeeding century.

This modest shaft marks the memorable spot where they withstood temptation and saved the State, but their monument is the Republic—its inscription upon the hearts of its teeming and happy millions.

www.ingramcontent.com/pod-product-compliance
Lightning Source LLC
Chambersburg PA
CBHW030408170426
43202CB00010B/1532